A CENTURY of AVIATION in NEW ZEALAND

The Twentieth Century

Paul Harrison & Brian Lockstone

Ballooning spans the century. At the end, it remains a popular pastime. At the beginning, it provided the means for the first aerial ascents in New Zealand. A crowd at Days' Bay, Wellington, watches this ascent by Capt. Noah Jonassen on 9 November 1907. *NAC collection*

Grantham House
New Zealand

Introduction

In these pictures and words we have endeavoured to capture the essence of aviation in New Zealand across the 20th century. More than any other mode of transport, aviation transformed the country. It brought the major cities within hours of one another and ended the isolation of the provinces. With the improvement in operating economics, particularly in the second half-century, came real savings, lowering air travel costs. It helped defend our shores and interests at home and in various parts of the world. It opened new forms of

W. M. Angus (right) with George Bolt gliding on the Cashmere Hills, Christchurch, in 1911. Angus later flew in the First World War, while Bolt went on to become Tasman Empire Airways Ltd's chief engineer. W.M. Angus, *Brian Lockstone collection*

economic activity, lifting the tourist industry to new heights. It helped transform the land and boost the country's primary production. Inevitably, we have not been able to include every aircraft type that has served our skies. Rather, we have selected those aircraft and events of the greatest significance, as New Zealanders took to the skies.

Paul Harrison, Brian Lockstone

Whether Richard Pearse made the first sustained, controlled flight will probably never be determined. What is beyond doubt is that he was a remarkable inventor. This is his final design, forerunner of today's short take-off and landing aircraft. Of note are the ailerons, for roll control, at either wing tip. *R.F. Macpherson*

Early aviators 3

Prominent among New Zealand's early aviators was J.W.H. Scotland (third from left) and his French-designed Caudron biplane which made its first flight at Otaki on 29 January 1914. In March of that year, he dropped the first, unofficial airmail over Temuka during a flight between Timaru and Christchurch. *R.F. Macpherson*

Left: The brothers Vivian and Leo Walsh are generally acknowledged to have made the first sustained, controlled flight in New Zealand in their Howard Wright biplane at Glenora Park, Papakura, on 5 February 1911. By 1913, the machine had been rebuilt after a crash, and Arthur Frederick Sandford, left, prepares for take-off with passenger W. Gissing. *Brian Lockstone collection*

Below: Almost forgotten these days are the exploits of the Wellington photographer Arthur Schaef whose monoplane *Vogel* took to the air in controlled hops at Lyall Bay, Wellington, as early as 1911. *Dominion Museum, NAC collection*

Lt Richard Bannerman transferred from the 1st New Zealand Expeditionary Force to the Royal Flying Corps during the First World War. Seen here with a French-built Spad during training in 1917, he shot down 15 enemy aircraft. He served in the RNZAF during the Second World War, rising to the rank of Air Commodore. *RNZAF Museum*

The New Zealand Flying School used a fleet of sea and floatplanes to train pilots for the First World War. Here, Curtiss flying boat "D" rests on its launching rails between flights at Mission Bay, Auckland. *Origin unknown; print provided by the late E.F. Harvie*

Canterbury Aviation Company staff and pupils with a Caudron two-seat trainer at Wigram in 1917. *RNZAF Museum*

New Zealand Flying School

Pigeons carried "airmails" between Great Barrier Island and Auckland in 1897. The NZFS promoted airmails, and the first official flight took place from Auckland to Dargaville and return on 16 December 1919. George Bolt was the pilot in a Boeing & Westerveldt single-engine seaplane when 825 letters and a parcel of newspapers were carried north and 1220 letters plus nine newspapers on the return. Bolt (right) hands a mail bag to the unidentified Dargaville postmaster (left) at the end of a flight on 9 and 10 April when mails were carried from Auckland to a number of Northland centres in a special flight organised by the region's champion, Colonel Allen Bell, appropriately dressed for the occasion. *E.F. Harvie collection, Brian Lockstone*

Below: The NZFS purchased the first two aircraft built by the Boeing Company at Lake Union, Seattle. These were large single-engine seaplanes powered by a six-cylinder, water-cooled Hall-Scott A-5 engine producing 125 hp at 1600 rpm, and they arrived by sea in October 1918. Here, "F" is about to lift off a tranquil Waitemata Harbour at Mission Bay. For years, rumours persisted that parts of these historic aircraft survived in tunnels under North Head, but it seems certain they were burned at the demise of NZFS in 1924. *E.F. Harvie collection*

Above: One of the prettiest early aircraft used by the NZFS was the Supermarine Channel flying boat. This arrived in Auckland in March 1921 and made several notable long-distance flights, including the first between Auckland and Wellington on 4 October 1921. Flown by George Bolt with two passengers, it made the journey in five hours and six minutes with stops at Kawhia and Wanganui. Here it is seen taxiing on Evans Bay, Wellington, with the old coal-fired power house, demolished after reconstruction of the city's airport in the 1950s, in the background. *E.F. Harvie collection*

Below: The Supermarine Channel at Mission Bay after its extensive rebuild following a visit by sea to Fiji where it had been used to survey the island group for the colonial administration in June-July 1921. Like the Boeing seaplanes, the Channel was sold for scrap in 1924. *E.F. Harvie collection*

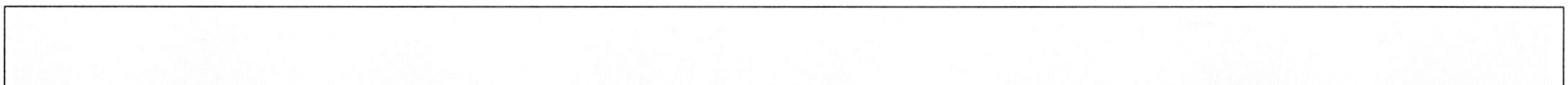

Early commercial flying

After the First World War, the NZFS acquired five Avro 504 biplanes, part of a consignment of military machines given by Britain to help establish an air force. The land versions were known as 504K and the seaplanes 504L. Here, H2990 carries joyriders at Shelly Beach, Auckland, in 1922. This particular machine was built, under contract, by the Brush Electrical Engineering Co Ltd and was taken over by the Permanent Air Force in 1924. *E.F. Harvie collection*

In 1926, Sir Henry Wigram donated £2,500 to buy an aeroplane for defence purposes. The Gloster Grebe fighter was chosen, and three were purchased from the RAF. They provided refresher training for ex-WWI pilots and were often seen at air displays. The diminutive fighters (wing span 8.94m, length 6.17m) were known for their noisy engines and stunning aerobatic manoeuvres, and with a top speed of 245 km/hr were the fastest aircraft in the country in the late 1920s. *RNZAF Museum*

Four of New Zealand's best-known aviators in front of an Avro 504K during the 1920s. Left to right: Capt. J.C. "Bert" Mercer, J.E. Moore, Capt. Euan Dickson and R.L. Wigley. Mercer founded Air Travel (NZ) Ltd, Dickson made the first flight across Cook Strait on 25 August 1920 in Avro 504K D6243, while Wigley pioneered alpine flying which led to the formation of what became Mount Cook Airlines. *J.C. Mercer collection*

Capt. J.C. Mercer brings a de Havilland 9 to a halt at One Tree Hill, Auckland, at the end of the first truly long-distance flight in New Zealand, from Invercargill to Auckland, on 24-25 October 1921. His passengers were R.L. Wigley, of Mount Cook fame, and W.H. Fleming, from the prominent South Island milling company. In perhaps the first form of aerial advertising, the dH 9 carried the name of one of the company's products, "Creamota", beneath its wings. *Mount Cook Airlines*

Capt. Euan Dickson (left) during a refuelling stop at Fairlie in his Avro 504K E4242 on the first attempt to fly to Mount Cook on 20 May 1920. *Mount Cook Airlines*

Left: The early aircraft were started the hard way. Two volunteers are starting the rotary engine of Avro 504K *Joybird* owned by L. Brake and J. Paul in the early 1930s. *Dudley Payne*

Below: The British manufacturer de Havilland produced some of the finest light aircraft between the two world wars and launched the aero club movement in several parts of the world. The Moth was perhaps the best known. Pictured is F. Douglas Mill with his (and New Zealand's) first, a DH 60X model, carrying the registration marks G-NZAT, at Hobsonville in July 1928. Mill formed the Air Survey & Transport Co Ltd which imported many Moths before the Second World War. *Brian Lockstone collection*

Possibly the oldest airworthy Moth is dH-60X G-EBLV, built in August 1928. It is pictured here with Ansett New Zealand's first British Aerospace 146 200 Series ZK-NZA at Hatfield, UK, in May 1989 before its ferry flight to New Zealand. The 146 carries UK test registration marks G-5-116. The captains who flew it to New Zealand were enthusiastic aviators and suggested at one point that they would swap the 146 for the Moth! Owners British Aerospace tactfully declined. The Moth now resides at the historic Shuttleworth Collection at Biggleswade. *Brian Lockstone*

Above: 11 September 1928 was a memorable day for New Zealand with the first successful Trans-Tasman flight by the Fokker F.VII *Southern Cross,* which landed at Wigram after a 14-hour, 15-minute flight from Sydney, flown by Charles Kingsford Smith and Charles Ulm. Scores of thousands greeted the flyers and several days later when this picture was taken, crowds were still admiring the aircraft. Two New Zealanders made up the crew, navigator H.A. Litchfield and wireless operator T.H. McWilliam. They returned on 13 October 1928, reaching Sydney 22 hours and 58 minutes after leaving Blenheim. *RNZAF Museum*

Opposite page – Top: New Zealand's first military aviation expedition was despatched in January 1930 to Samoa, where violence had been directed at the administration. Under a League of Nations mandate, New Zealand was responsible for Samoa, and the Government sent HMS *Dunedin* to help quell the disturbances. Embarked was a New Zealand Permanent Air Force Gipsy Moth "995", with Flight Lieutenant Sidney Wallingford and two mechanics. Based at Apia, the Moth flew over 90 hours, dropping leaflets and carrying out reconnaissance. On one occasion, it dropped a home-made bomb onto a suspect vessel. Fortunately, it failed to explode for the vessel was a missionary craft en route between islands. The Moth is seen here on its cradle on the shores of Apia. *G.S. Wallingford*

Above: From 1929, New Zealand civil aircraft carried registration marks beginning with the prefix "ZK". The British oil company millionaire Sir Charles Wakefield presented DH-60G ZK-AAA to the Marlborough Aero Club, which painted his name on the machine in gratitude. Alongside is a dH-60G of the NZ Permanent Air Force. *Brian Lockstone collection*

Opposite page – Lower: From the earliest days of the aero club movement, air shows, then known as pageants, were popular. Pictured here is a gathering of Moths at Mangere, now buried under the present Auckland International Airport, in January 1931. At left is a New Zealand Permanent Air Force Moth and centre right, one of the Auckland Aero Club's distinctively marked Moths. *Brian Lockstone collection*

Aero Clubs formed

Left: The New Plymouth Aero Club was one of the early birds, leasing a farm at Bell Block, north of the city. This 1929 picture shows two visiting Moths, ZK-AAE and AAO, from the Auckland Aero Club. The former was a gift from the *New Zealand Herald* newspaper. The airfield was later named Bell Block. *Brian Lockstone collection*

George Bolt made New Zealand's first recorded glider flight in 1911. Between the wars, the gliding movement became established. W.M. Angus is pictured at the controls of a Zogling primary trainer at Timaru in 1931. *W.M. Angus*

Sir Charles Kingsford Smith and the *Southern Cross* made their final visit to New Zealand in 1934. On 13 January he flew from Sydney to New Plymouth in 15 hours and 25 minutes. This group includes leading lights in the aero club and reception committee. Kingsford Smith is eighth from the left. Immediately beneath the vertical propeller blade on the central engine is his navigator, P.G. (Bill) Taylor, and on his left wireless operator John Stannage. Seated centre is Percy V. Stainton, who served as chairman of the New Plymouth Airport Board for several years. *Brian Lockstone collection*

First rotary-wing flight

Maritime aviation in the NZPAF, and later the RNZAF, was based at Hobsonville in the upper reaches of the Waitemata Harbour. The main aircraft used were seaplanes. Seen here is Fairey IIIF "F.1133" on the water astern of HMS *Diomede* during annual exercises at Whangaroa in March 1933. The inset photograph shows Fairey IIIB "S1805", being launched at Hobsonville. *RNZN Museum; inset G.S. Wallingford collection*

The first rotary-wing flight in New Zealand took place in January 1931 when this Cierva C19 Mk III autogyro, imported by Garland & Grant Ltd, was test-flown at Wigram by Flt Lt Bob Matheson. Unlike the helicopter, the autogyro's rotor was free-wheeling, other than a clutch for start-up, with the main power generated by the engine and propeller. *Brian Lockstone collection*

Above: A Canterbury Aero Club Moth, flown by Capt. J.C. Mercer passing over Whitcombe Pass in September 1933, when two tourists were flown to Franz Josef. *Brian Lockstone collection*

The first new aircraft ordered for the RNZAF in 1934 were Vickers Vildebeeste biplane bombers. The first 12 were delivered in 1936 and formed the first operational unit of the RNZAF. With the outbreak of war looming in 1938, Vickers Vincents, a similar design to the Vildebeestes, were ordered for general reconnaissance work and training. The photograph below shows the first of the second-hand RAF Vincents at Hobsonville shortly after arrival in July 1939. The nearest aircraft, K6361, became NZ309. The photograph on the left, shows one of the first Vildebeestes, NZ103, over Auckland. *RNZAF Museum, P.A. Harrison collection*

Overseas visitors

For his 1933-35 Antarctic expedition, the noted US explorer Rear Admiral Richard Byrd used four aircraft, including this Curtiss-Wright T-32 Condor, being unloaded on the Wellington wharves. At the time, this was the most modern airliner to be seen in New Zealand. Similar models were used by American Airlines and Eastern Air Transport on early sleeper flights across the US. *Brian Lockstone collection*

Scheduled airlines got under way in the mid-1930s with East Coast Airways, then Union Airways, the first into service. Here, a UA de Havilland 86 Express airliner is loaded prior to departure. *NAC*

Below: Pan American was the first to span the South Pacific with this Sikorsky S-42 *Samoa Clipper*, commanded by Capt. Edwin C. Musick in March 1937. The S-42 drew thousands of spectators to Mechanics Bay, Auckland. *Pan American historical collection*

Above: By late 1938 the RNZAF was in a transition stage of retiring the most elderly aircraft and was bringing into service interim second-hand RAF aeroplanes to fill the need for the expansion training then under way. Showing that transition is this photograph taken at Hobsonville. The aircraft and their periods of service with the NZPAF/RNZAF are from left to right: de Havilland DH60 Moth (1929-1936), FAIREY IIIF (1929-1939), Blackburn Baffin (1937-1941) and the Gloster Grebe (1928-1938). *RNZAF Official*

Left: While the British were still building biplanes, the American industry was producing speedy monoplanes such as this Rearwin 9000L Sportster, assembled at Mangere in 1938 for delivery to the Te Kuiti Aero Club. *Brian Lockstone collection*

Below: Throughout the war years, the de Havilland DH82A Tiger Moth was the primary trainer for *ab initio* pilots. A total of 335 Tiger Moths was to see service with the RNZAF between 1939 and 1956. The Tiger Moths were a mixture of ex-RAF machines and those built locally at the de Havilland factory at Rongotai in Wellington. This facility became the domestic air terminal from 1959 to 1999. This photograph shows a line-up of yellow Tiger Moths at No.3 Elementary Flying School (Harewood) with a mixture of markings typical of the early wartime period. *RNZAF Museum*

TEAL begins operations

Above: For seven years from 1940, Tasman Empire Airways Ltd's fleet consisted of two Short S.30 flying boats, *Aotearoa* and *Awarua*, seen here at anchor at Mechanics Bay in 1940. Carrying 19 passengers, they maintained the vital wartime link with Sydney, flew the occasional maritime surveillance patrols and were broken up on retirement. *Auckland Star*

Below: The first Short flying boat to visit New Zealand, however, was Imperial Airways' S.23 *Centaurus* which made a survey flight from Britain at the instigation of Colonel N.S. Falla, chairman of the Union Steam Ship Co Ltd (and later Union Airways). Commanded by New Zealander Capt. John Burgess, it arrived in Auckland on 27 December 1937, later visiting Wellington, Lyttelton and Dunedin, where it is pictured, on 3 January 1938. *Leonard Lockstone*

Below: Pan American World Airways used the Sikorsky S-42 for route proving in the southern Pacific, waiting until the immense Boeing 314 became available to start scheduled services. The *California Clipper* was the first to arrive, on 30 August 1939. *Paul Harrison collection*

In 1939, New Zealand airmen were in the UK to collect 30 new Wellington bombers on order for the RNZAF. At the outbreak of war, the New Zealand Government transferred these aircraft and their crews to the RAF where they became No.75 Squadron. They had a remarkable wartime record, flying Wellingtons, Stirlings and finally Lancasters over occupied Europe and Germany. One pilot, Sergeant James Ward, was awarded the Victoria Cross, and many others collected decorations for gallantry and outstanding service. The main photograph shows the effects of a No.75 Squadron bombing sortie on a German-occupied airfield at St Trond, Belgium, on 15 August 1944. The inset shows a Lancaster of the squadron's "A" Flight being prepared for a night sortie over Germany in late 1944. *Paul Harrison collection*

Maritime aviation continued during the war years with Hobsonville being the primary training centre for this form of military activity in New Zealand. A Walrus amphibian used for pilot conversion forms the backdrop to this 1943 scene showing how airmen were trained in basic seamen skills, vital for maritime aviators. *RNZAF Museum*

The Pacific War   19

The first of the modern training aircraft to reach New Zealand under the Commonwealth air training plan was the North American Harvard in 1941. These became a familiar sight and sound over the next 36 years, and a total of 202 saw service. Here, a flight of newly delivered Harvards from No.1 Services Flying Training School at Wigram is seen near the Port Hills in late 1941. *RNZAF Museum*

The first Lockheed Hudsons arrived in New Zealand in April 1941. Serving with No.3 Squadron, they were the first RNZAF aircraft to directly engage the Japanese, at Guadalcanal, in late November 1942. A Mk5 (NZ2001) is seen here in early 1942 when operated by No.1 General Reconnaissance (GR) Squadron at Whenuapai. *RNZAF Museum*

RNZAF Curtiss P-40 Warhawks undergoing servicing in the Solomon Islands. Between 1941 and 1943, the P-40 was the RNZAF's Pacific front-line fighter, and No.15 Squadron, which moved to Guadalcanal in April 1943, was the first to engage the enemy. The NZ Fighter wing shot down 99 Japanese aircraft. As they were replaced by newer P-40s and eventually the Corsair, many of the veterans returned to New Zealand for use by the Fighter Operational Training Units. *RNZAF Museum*

The Lockheed Ventura medium bomber was introduced into service in mid-1943. Six RNZAF Squadrons operated them for bombing and for patrol work around the Northern Solomon Islands. Here, a flight of Venturas is about to be loaded with bombs at Green Island, prior to a raid on Rabaul. *RNZAF Museum*

Acquired as torpedo bombers, the Grumman Avengers of the RNZAF were to see service as dive-bombers with Nos 30 and 31 Squadrons. The two squadrons each made a single tour of operations at Bougainville in 1944. The RNZAF used 48 Avengers, and after the war two were used for topdressing proving trials. These new arrivals for No.30 Squadron, based at Darton Field, Gisborne, are on a cross-country flight near the East Coast. *RNZAF Museum*

Another of the New Zealand squadrons was No.489 of RAF Coastal Command which flew Blenheims, then Hampdens, Beaufighters and finally Mosquitos. One duty was to harass and sink German shipping plying the western approaches and around Norway, as part of the ANZAC Wing, with a sister squadron of Australian Beaufighters at Dallachy in Scotland in 1944. Here, a No.489 (NZ) Squadron Beaufighter (coded P6-6) is escorted by a Mustang of No.315 (Polish) Squadron. *RNZAF*

The Pacific War

Catalina flying boats provided the RNZAF with the ability to watch vast areas of the south-west and South Pacific, looking for Japanese submarines and surface vessels. They also provided a valuable service with several notable rescues of downed airmen and survivors from sunken Allied vessels. Main operational base for No.6 Squadron was at Halavo Bay on Florida Island north of Guadalcanal, where this Catalina is about to be brought up from the water for maintenance in July 1944. *RNZAF Museum*

At its wartime peak, the RNZAF had nearly 15,000 personnel in the south-west Pacific forward area. Supporting this sizeable force was No.40 Squadron with Douglas Dakotas, which flew long distances with great efficiency and organisation. A second Dakota squadron was formed, and after the war many were transferred to the new National Airways Corporation as DC-3s. Homeward-bound is a load of RNZAF airmen enjoying the basic comfort of a wartime Dakota. *RNZAF Museum*

More Chance Vought Corsairs served in the wartime RNZAF than any other aircraft. A total of 424 was used for four years from 1944 in 13 squadrons. Designed as a naval fighter, the robust and fast Corsair was well liked by its pilots. This photograph shows a section of No.18 (Fighter) Squadron RNZAF Corsairs off the coast of Guadalcanal. *RNZAF Museum*

During the war, over 1,000 New Zealanders flew in the Royal Navy's Fleet Air Arm. Kiwi Seafire pilots from a Royal Navy carrier are seen here visiting their RNZAF counterparts at Mokerang airfield on Manus Island in the Admiralty Islands in mid-1945. *RNZAF Museum*

TEAL replaced its S.30s, which carried only 19 passengers, with four Tasman-class Short Sandringhams, converted from wartime Sunderlands. The 30-passenger aircraft had a chequered career with one, *New Zealand*, almost lost because of engine overheating problems. They remained in service only four years. Here, ZK-AMH is prepared for service at Mechanics Bay. *Paul Harrison collection*

The reliable and much-loved Short S.45 Solent succeeded the Sandringham. The TEAL fleet consisted of one 39-passenger Mk III and four 45-passenger Mk IVs, which flew Tasman and Pacific routes. The last Solent, *Aranui*, pictured on the Waitemata Harbour, maintained the Coral Route until 1960 before retiring to MOTAT. *Air New Zealand*

Above: The Solents also provided Wellington's first international air services, operating from Evans Bay, Wellington, to Rose Bay in Sydney. In this photograph Solent ZK-AMM awaits its passengers before departing for Sydney. In the foreground are the launches that swept the alighting area, assisted with mooring and provided air traffic control services. *Jack Browne*

TEAL's first flight attendants (first called stewardesses, then hostesses) were left to right: B.P. Morton, V. Beckett, L.M. Magnus, D.C. Everard, J. Paterson and P.M. Woolley, lined up at Mechanics Bay. *Air New Zealand*

Interim years

Above: With the war over, the need for hundreds of aircraft disappeared. Surplus aircraft were flown to Rukuhia and other storage areas, where they were progressively stripped of useful parts, then cut up into manageable chunks for the roaring aluminium smelters constructed to turn them into material for civilian industry. Here, Venturas and Avengers await their fate at Rukuhia in 1947. *RNZAF Museum*

Above: With the end of the war and the lend-lease agreement with the United States, New Zealand turned back to Britain as a source of aircraft. Eighty de Havilland Mosquito fighter bombers and trainers were acquired, but only a handful saw service with No.75 Squadron, using the famous wartime "number plate" from 1946 to 1952, and No.14 Squadron briefly in 1949. Most were flown straight into long-term storage at Woodbourne. In 1952, they were replaced by another shapely de Havilland product, the Vampire jet fighter. *RNZAF*

Rocket-firing North American Mustang IV fighters of the Territorial Air Force. In 1945, the RNZAF planned to replace its Corsairs with the famed Mustang. With the war's sudden end in August 1945, the order was cancelled. However, 30 were already on the water and on arrival were placed into storage. With the reactivation of the Territorial Air Force in 1949, they were brought into service for the four TAF fighter squadrons. When the TAF was disbanded in 1956, they were retired, with the exception of four which served with No.42 Squadron for a short period, towing targets for Vampires, amongst other duties. *RNZAF Museum*

At the end of the war, the British, Australian and Canadian governments set up British Commonwealth Pacific Airlines, based in Australia, to span the Pacific with four Douglas DC-6s. One was lost on approach to San Francisco, and the others were transferred to TEAL when BCPA was wound up in 1954. BCPA's VH-BPE *Resolution* took part in the official opening of Christchurch Airport in 1948. *Brian Lockstone collection*

The National Airways Corporation was formed after the war from the pre-war Union Airways and smaller airlines. Until the arrival of the DC-3, Lockheed airliners formed the backbone of the fleet. At left and right are two Electras, flanking two bigger Lodestars, pictured at Paraparaumu, home to NAC while Wellington airport was reconstructed. At the far left is Electra *Kaka*, lost on Mt Ruapehu on 23 October 1948, with 13 killed. *Photo News/NAC*

While the flying boats had great sentimental appeal, airlines needed the greater speed and productivity of the land plane. In 1954, TEAL replaced its Solents on all but the Pacific routes with three Douglas DC-6s. Here, one is refuelled at Whenuapai prior to boarding passengers for Sydney. The last TEAL DC-6 was still flying, as a fire-fighting tanker, in the 1980s. *Brian Lockstone*

Interim years

Pan American World Airways was the first foreign airline to fly to New Zealand after the Second World War, first using DC-4s then the mighty Boeing 377 Stratocruiser. Whenuapai served as Auckland's international airport until 1965. The double-decker Stratocruiser was developed from the B-29 bomber. Popular with passengers was the bar on the lower deck. The airliner provided luxury connections to San Francisco via Fiji, Canton Is and Hawaii. *Don Noble collection*

Two Curtiss C-46 Commando freighters, from Taiwan's Civil Air Transport and pictured at Whenuapai, were chartered to move cargo across Cook Strait during the 1951 waterfront strike. *Brian Lockstone collection*

de Havilland's shapely 8/10 seater, DH89, served NAC with distinction on regional routes from inception until December 1963. Pre-war models were called Rapides, while those built for Air Force use during the war were known as Domines. *NAC collection*

By the mid-1950s, NAC had standardised on the DC-3 airliner, pictured lifting off from New Plymouth's old Bell Block airfield. *Alf Brandon, Brian Lockstone collection*

The RNZAF's first operational jet fighter was the de Havilland Vampire with its distinctive twin tail booms. A total of 58 single-seater and dual-seat trainers was flown variously by No.14 and 75 Squadrons between 1952 and 1972. Precise formation aerobatics made them popular at air shows. *RNZAF Museum*

Military and civil long range aircraft

The first truly long-range transport aircraft for the RNZAF were the four Handley Page Hastings C.3 transports introduced in 1952. First with No.41 Squadron, then No.40 Squadron, these four-engine aircraft crossed the world in support of RNZAF and Government tasks. The aircraft had a tail wheel configuration and were not the most useful for carrying large loads. They were withdrawn from service in 1965 and broken up for scrap at Ohakea. NZ5802 is seen here at Nausori, Fiji, on 1 March 1965. *RNZAF Museum*

Above: Qantas launched landplane international services into Wellington with Sydney-Wellington flights on 3 October 1961 with Lockheed L.188C Electra turbo-props. Here, founder and chairman Sir Hudson Fysh receives a formal Maori welcome. *Qantas*

Left: To mark the occasion of the first Qantas service into Wellington, Sir Hudson Fysh (right) presented the clock from the Short S.23 *Centaurus*, which had flown the Imperial Airways survey flight in December 1937. On hand was New Zealander Capt. John Burgess (second from right) who commanded that flight and later represented British Overseas Airways Corporation in Australia. At left are Hon J.K. McAlpine, Minister of Transport, and the Rt Hon Sir Walter Nash, Leader of the Opposition. *Qantas*

Above: The scene at Wellington Airport in August 1962 when a guard of honour greeted the arrival of HM King Bhumiphol Adulyadey and Queen Sirikit of Thailand after their arrival in a Qantas Lockheed Electra from Australia. On the other side of the airport, clouds of smoke signal a 21-gun royal salute. *Qantas*

Right: Described by an American in Vietnam as the "packing box the aircraft came in", the chunky lines of the Bristol Freighter Mk31M were often the butt of derogatory remarks over their 26 years of flying with the RNZAF from 1951. The 12 Freighters proved to be useful transports and are primarily associated with No.41 Squadron, based in Singapore from 1955 to 1977. *RNZAF Museum*

Below: The Short Sunderland flying boats were first introduced to the RNZAF in 1944, when four MK III transports were flown from Britain for South Pacific transport runs. In 1953, 16 refurbished ex-RAF MR5s began delivery to the RNZAF. Flying with No.5 Squadron in Fiji, these graceful four-engine flying boats quickly earned a reputation for medical evacuations, search and rescue and communications tasks around the South Pacific. Seen here is a Sunderland NZ4107 (D) with a Marlin flying boat (USN) and a Neptune (RAAF) during an exercise in the Philippines in the early 1960s. *RNZAF Museum*

Foreign Affairs

The RNZAF formed the Antarctic flight to support the 1957 Commonwealth Trans-Antarctic Expedition. It was equipped with a de Havilland DHC2 Beaver and an Auster T.7c an ex-RAF machine. This little aircraft accompanied the expedition on HMNZS *Endeavour* on the journey to McMurdo Sound in December 1956. On floats, then skis, the Auster was kept busy during the summer of 1957, with reconnaissance missions and carrying parties of scientists to various locations around McMurdo Sound and the Ross Sea ice shelf. During the winter months at Scott Base (near McMurdo), the Auster was buried in a snow cave, flying as weather permitted. Shipped home after the summer season of 1958, it returned south for the 1959/60 summer. This Auster is now displayed in the RNZAF Museum at Wigram, Christchurch. The RNZAF operated seven Austers between 1947 and 1970. *RNZAF Museum*

Above: The Canterbury international air race was held between 10 and 11 October 1953 with a fleet of aircraft racing from the United Kingdom to Christchurch. The speed section was fought out by RAF and RAAF Canberras. Winner of the transport section, however, was a KLM Douglas DC-6A under the command of Capt. Han A.A. Kooper and a crew of 10. The airliner carried 55 Dutch migrants, together with representatives of the media and the Douglas company. Here, Capt. Kooper receives his prize from the Governor-General, Sir Willoughby Norrie. Seated at right is the Leader of the Opposition, Rt Hon Sir Walter Nash. *New Zealand Government*

Below: NAC entered the gas turbine era in 1958 with the Vickers Viscount. Its four Rolls Royce Dart turbo-prop engines, high cruising speed, superior cabin appointments and service, with above-the-turbulence cruising altitudes, transformed domestic air travel. Here, City of Wellington prepares to depart the capital's airport. *NAC collection*

Agrian pursuits

Above: New Plymouth's Rural Aviation Ltd was one of the country's earliest aerial topdressing companies. The company imported Cessna products, including this model C.180 working off Ngamotu Beach in the mid-1950s. In the background is Paritutu Rock, one of the Sugarloaf Rocks. Today the skyline has been transformed by a thermal power station, while the beach is all but buried by industrial development. *Brian Lockstone*

Above right: The Piper Pawnee was popular with aerial topdressing companies. Pictured here is Aerial Farming of NZ Ltd's machine loading at a strip near Omata, Taranaki, in 1966. Many surviving Pawnees were converted to glider-towing duties. *Brian Lockstone*

Right: The British manufacturer Auster Aircraft Ltd designed the Agricola aerial topdresser with the New Zealand market in mind. It found the competition hard going, but its operators always liked the sturdy machine. This example is working off a strip behind Paekakariki in the early 1970s – landing uphill and taking off down. *Brian Lockstone*

Right: The de Havilland Canada Beaver was one of the workhorses of the aerial topdressing fleet. A Fieldair Ltd example undergoes servicing at Gisborne, engine cowlings in the foreground. *Brian Lockstone*

Agrian pursuits

Te Kuiti-based Bennett Aviation Ltd produced two unconventional Airtrucks, from a design by Italian Luigi Pellarini, making extensive use of Harvard components. The model was eventually developed into the PL11 Aitruk. *Brian Lockstone collection*

Above: Cornerstone of the aerial topdressing industry over the last 40 years has been the Fletcher Fu-24 in various versions. Here an Fu-24 950 is hard at work near Gladstone in the Wairarapa during 1999. *Brian Lockstone*

The business end of the Fu-24 950's hopper in action. *Brian Lockstone*

Above: The first English Electric Canberra B(I)12 bombers entered service with No.14 Squadron at Ohakea in late 1959. Based at Ohakea, the squadron regularly deployed to Australia, Fiji and South-East Asia. Of the 11 bombers and two T.13 trainers, only two were lost between 1959 and 1970. Three Canberra B(I)12s are shown low over the coast of Singapore. *RNZAF Museum*

Above right: Warbirds – restored ex-military aircraft – are now an active part of the New Zealand aviation world. The first such was "Charlie Charlie Golf", an ex-RNZAF Territorial Air Force Mustang fighter restored by Ron Fechney and Jack McDonald during the 1960s, and seen here at New Plymouth's Bell Block airfield in the mid-1960s when it was flown by the late Jack McDonald. It remains airworthy in the USA. *Brian Lockstone*

Bell Sioux joined No.3 Squadron in 1965, the first helicopters to be operated by the Air Force. Thirteen were acquired, and today the last five are used for conversion training. Here, a standard skid and a float-equipped Sioux are seen over a lake during an exercise. *RNZAF Museum*

Heavy lift helicopters 33

The first Boeing 747 to visit New Zealand was this Qantas model 238 in January 1972. It is seen here at Auckland with a National Airways Corporation Boeing 737 for comparison.
Auckland Star, Brian Lockstone collection

For 35 years, the Bell Iroquois has served the RNZAF around the world, in the UK, South-East Asia, the Antarctic and, more recently, on peace-keeping duties in Bougainville and East Timor. Five UH-1Ds joined No.3 Squadron, followed in 1970 by nine UH-1H versions. During the 1970s the 1Ds were upgraded to UH-1H standard. This is an early shot of UH-1D NZ3804 delivering a practice underslung load in the local training area at Hobsonville.
RNZAF Museum

Above: Mount Cook airlines acquired the assets of Tourist Air Travel Ltd, including its fleet of Grumman Widgeon amphibians, one of which is seen taking off on the Waitemata Harbour in 1971. Under the command of Capt. Fred Ladd, the Widgeons were much loved around the Hauraki Gulf, performing countless mercy flights and providing vital links with the mainland. *Brian Lockstone*

Above right: The Taranaki Glider Club's first machine, a two-seat Schleicher Rhönlerche II Ka-4, is readied for launch. *Brian Lockstone*

Below: This Schleicher Rhönsegler captures the essence of gliding in this study of light and shade above the hills near Ardmore in the late 1960s. *Brian Lockstone*

Mount Cook Airlines | 35

Above: Ever since the 1937 Cochrane Report, a primary function of the RNZAF has been the protection of our sea lanes and the approaches to New Zealand. Five Orions joined No.5 Squadron in 1966, followed by an ex-RAAF version in 1984. Here, Orion NZ4203 is in its element during the late 1980s. *RNZAF Official*

Left: Mount Cook Airlines became a legend for its alpine flying expertise. Its first glacier landing took place in September 1955 using this Auster J/1B Aiglet. On the 20th anniversary, Mt Cook managing director Sir Harry Wigley (on the right in the lower photograph) and pilot A. McWhirter recreated the occasion in the same Auster. *Mount Cook Airlines*

When Air New Zealand bought the Lockheed Electra in 1959, it was said that Qantas, then a shareholder, had exercised its powers at board level to persuade the airline not to buy jet airliners. Whether true or not, this led to the claim that TEAL actually stood for "Take Electras And Like it"! The reliable Electras remained in service until 1971 when their last duties were to operate joint services out of Wellington for Air New Zealand and Qantas, hence the dual inscription on the fuselage. *Brian Lockstone*

Above: The RNZAF's Lockheed C-130H Hercules transports have served around the world, from the sub-zero temperatures of the Antarctic to the searing desert heat of the Gulf War. Their tasks have ranged from support for New Zealand operations across Asia to combat support flights in the Gulf War (1990/91), support missions to Somalia (1993), Bougainville (1997), the Kosovo crisis (1998) and East Timor. In addition are countless disaster relief and humanitarian operations near and far, and community and Government tasks within New Zealand. Hercules NZ7003 departs a desert airfield during the Gulf War. *RNZAF Official*

US manufacturer Cessna produced a line of high-wing, single-engined aircraft which became trend-setters for the rest of the industry. Seagulls sun themselves on this Floatplane Air Services Cessna U206G on Lake Rotorua in April 1983. *Gavin Woodward*

The big airliners

Left: A crowd of well-wishers surrounds the first of seven DC-8-52 airliners operated by Air New Zealand at Auckland airport in 1965. The Douglas was selected ahead of the Boeing 707, the Comet IV and Vickers VC-10 and remained in the fleet until 1989, when the last, a freighter, was sold. *Anthony Henry/Air New Zealand*

Below: Qantas bought the Boeing 747SP, a cut-back version of the standard 200 Series Jumbo, for services into Wellington and other challenging routes. Here, VH-EAB is about to touch down on its inaugural flight on 31 January 1981. Rising terrain to the north of the capital imposed special demands on aircraft performance. *Brian Lockstone*

Before the advent of Ansett New Zealand in 1987, passengers had to struggle up and down steps and trudge through the often inclement weather between aircraft and terminal. Happily, for these passengers leaving an Air New Zealand DC-8 at Wellington airport in 1973 after a flight from Australia, it is a fine day. *Brian Lockstone*

For the past 30 years the McDonnell Douglas A-4 Skyhawk has equipped the RNZAF's Air Attack Force. Fourteen single-seat A-4Ks and two-seat TA-4Ks were delivered by ship in October 1970. Serving with No.75 Squadron, they have become familiar sights around New Zealand, Australia and South-East Asia. A further 10 ex-RAN Skyhawks were purchased in 1984. This allowed the formation of a second Skyhawk squadron, No.2 Squadron, which has been based at the Royal Australian Naval Air Station at Nowra, NSW, Australia, since 1991. A-4K NZ6201 on the flight line at Ohakea in February 1997. *RNZAF Official*

Right: Airlines have quaint old habits, such as this ceremonial snipping of Air New Zealand Capt. Phil Le Couteur's tie at Long Beach, California, to mark the handover of the airline's first McDonnell Douglas DC-10-30 in 1973. The "surgeon" is Charles Forsyth, vice-president of marketing for the manufacturer. Enjoying the moment at left is Cyril Keppel, later chief executive officer at the airline. Air New Zealand ran a fleet of 8 DC-10-30s, the last retiring in 1983. *McDonnell Douglas*

Left: Bay of Plenty Airways Ltd operated this de Havilland Dove during the 1960s on services to Auckland. A design feature of the Dove (civil cousin of the military Devon) was the sawn-off port tailplane which improved handling in the event of the loss of an engine. *Brian Lockstone*

Regional airlines

During the 1970s, British Airways operated Air New Zealand's DC-10-30 trijets between Los Angeles and London before New Zealand had traffic rights into the British capital. In between flights at Heathrow are ZK-NZS and NZT. *Fred Barnes*

Small airlines have always struggled in New Zealand because of the small market and high operating costs. One such was Trans Island Airways which operated this pre-war Lockheed Electra, pictured awaiting passengers at Christchurch Airport in the 1960s. *Brian Lockstone*

Another small airline was Rotorua-based Air North, which had a mixed fleet including this ex-National Airways Corporation de Havilland Heron, seen at Auckland Airport unloading passengers in the early 1970s. *Brian Lockstone*

National Airways Corporation made extensive use of the Fokker F.27 Friendship, which replaced DC-3s during the 1960s as the country's regional airports were brought up to date with modern approach and landing aids and sealed runways. Fifteen years separate these two pictures with NAC's second F.27, (upper), a 100 Series at Wellington Airport, unloading passengers recently arrived from Auckland in 1961, and (above), a 500 Series, with its distinctive forward cargo door, at Napier. *Brian Lockstone*

Above: Venison became a prized export during the 1960s and '70s. A Bell 206 Jetranger of Alpine Helicopters Ltd brings another shipment of deer in for processing. *Brian Lockstone*

Left: During the 1960s and '70s, search and rescue was provided at Auckland Airport by this Saunders Roe SRN5 Hovercraft, which could surface-skim water and mudflats on the Manukau Harbour. *Brian Lockstone*

Tiger Moths continue flying

Nearly 70 years on, the Tiger Moth is still with us. After wartime service, it returned to the aero clubs and helped found the aerial topdressing industry. *Dept of Agriculture* When the aero clubs switched to cabin aircraft, Tigers became prized objects in the hands of private owners. Some had canopies to protect their occupants (lower right), such as this model at Bell Block in the mid-1960s. The purists preferred the open air (upper right), with this example set for take-off at Napier in the 1970s. *Brian Lockstone*

Left: One of the oldest aircraft still flying in New Zealand is this pretty little pre-war Piper J-3C-50 Cub, based at Masterton. *Brian Lockstone*

Lower: In the 1950s and '60s, later model Cubs were active in the aerial topdressing and spraying industry, including this example demonstrating its capabilities at an air show at Wanganui. *Jim Kilsby*

Ansett New Zealand launched their service in 1987 with a fleet of Boeing 737-100 Series, almost two metres shorter and lighter than Air New Zealand's 200 Series. *Ansett New Zealand*

Ansett New Zealand used three versions of the British Aerospace 146: the 200 and longer 300 Series and the 200QC convertible. They called them Whisper Jets. Originally acquired for jet services into Queenstown (pictured), they were also pressed into service on the main routes. *Brian Lockstone*

The reshaping of regional airliner services in the 1980s brought new shapes to New Zealand skies, including the advanced Saab 340 turbo-prop, pictured at Wellington. It was acquired by Air Nelson and later sold to Air New Zealand to operate as part of its Link network. *Peter Clark*

Boeing 737s in action 43

During the 1980s, Air New Zealand fitted the 737s with hush-kits onto the rear sections of the engine nacelles, to lower noise on take-off and landing. *Brian Lockstone*

Air New Zealand began replacing the early 200 series Boeing 737 with a larger model, illustrated by this colourfully marked model 33R seen landing at Christchurch Airport during 1998. *Brian Lockstone*

Fiji's Air Pacific introduced the latest Boeing 737 model, the Next Generation 800, on services into New Zealand during 1999. This model has a longer fuselage and a redesigned wing which flies it further and faster than earlier models. *Brian Lockstone*

Over the post-war years the RNZAF operated a variety of light and medium transport aircraft. Between 1951 and 1981, 30 de Havilland Devons were used for training pilots, navigators and signallers along with communications duties. In 1981 they were replaced by Cessna Golden Eagles on communications duties until 1991. In 1976, 10 Hawker Siddeley Andover CMk1 twin-engine tactical transports were bought from the RAF. They served as tactical transports with No.1 Squadron between 1976 and 1984, while No.42 Squadron used them for VIP and general transport duties between1977 and 1998. From 1988 to 1990 an Andover was based at Teheran as part of the United Nations International Military Observers Group (UNIMOG), monitoring the cease-fire between Iran and Iraq. Between January and May 1993, three Andovers, their crews and support personnel were based at Mogadishu Airport, Somalia, in support of the US-led military coalition, UNITAF. In this formation, a VIP Andover leads the last Devon with Cessna Golden Eagle in the middle position. *RNZAF Official*

The RNZAF flew 19 Pacific Aerospace Corp. CT/4B *ab-initio* trainers, which entered service at Wigram in late 1976. The "Red Checkers" aerobatic team was formed in 1980, providing thrilling precision formation flying. In 1998 the CT/4Bs were replaced with 13 leased CT/4E Airtrainers, an improved version of this New Zealand-built aircraft. A newly delivered Airtrainer NZ1936 is seen over Wigram in early 1977. *RNZAF Official*

Air Chathams Ltd uses this Convair 580 to provide cargo and passenger links with Wellington and Christchurch. The turbo-prop 580 was developed from the earlier Convair 440. Other 580s provide overnight freight services between Auckland and Christchurch. *Brian Lockstone*

Commercial varieties 45

Helicopters have become a vital part of the aviation business. This Helipro Bell UH-1G Huey carries an aerial fire-fighting bucket. *Brian Lockstone*

Below: To mark the 50th anniversary of the first aerial crossing of the Tasman in 1978, this Fletcher Fu 24 made the crossing under the command of round-the-world flier Cliff Tait. The ZK-USU registration marks commemorated the VH-USU registration of the Southern Cross (although not carried on its 1928 flights). *Gavin Woodward*

One of two bulbous Carvairs bought by Nationwide Air for a short-lived, car-carrying venture in the 1970s. The aircraft was converted from the Douglas DC-4 airliner. *Brian Lockstone*

A USAF Lockheed C-141A Starlifter at Auckland airport. This military transport became a frequent visitor to Christchurch from the 1970s when it took over heavy haulage duties in support of the US and Allied Antarctic expeditions. *NAC*

Another long-serving airliner was the DC-3 replacement Hawker Siddeley 748, first operated by Mount Cook Airlines in 1968. A dual nose-wheel undercarriage enabled it to use semi-prepared airfields. During the 1970s, the airline spread its tourist network from its southern alpine base to Rotorua, where passengers board Aorangi in the early 1970s. *New Zealand Government*

Mainstay of Air New Zealand's long-haul fleet is the Boeing 747-400 (pictured). The airline uses two engine types: the Rolls Royce RB211-524G and the General Electric GE CF6-80C2B1F. *Air New Zealand – electronic image*

For regional routes, Air New Zealand uses the Franco-Italian ATR-72. This ultra-efficient 66-seater is powered by two Pratt & Whitney Canada PW127 turbo-props. *Air New Zealand – electronic image*

The last jets to join the RNZAF inventory in the 20th Century were 18 Aermacchi MB339CB jet trainers which replaced the BAC Strikemaster, in service since 1972. Since 1991, No.14 Squadron at Ohakea has used the Macchi for advanced and lead-in training for pilots selected to fly Skyhawks. This picture illustrates the transition from Strikemaster (left) with a new Macchi MB339CB in the foreground. *RNZAF Official*

More than any other fighter, the Spitfire evokes the dash and daring of the Second World War Commonwealth and Allied fighter pilot. No.485 (NZ) Squadron flew Spitfires during the war. Leading Warbird exponent Sir Tim Wallis owns this late-war Mk XVI, which actually served with an Australian squadron. Based at Wanaka in the South Island, it salutes the many hundreds of young New Zealand pilots who served their country in Fighter Command. *Paul Harrison*